PREPARE
— FOR —
IMPACT

JEFF BOESEL

Copyright © 2022 by Jeffrey D Boesel

All Rights Reserved.

No part of this book may be used or reproduced by any means, graphic, electronic, or mechanical, including photocopying, recording, taping, or by any information storage retrieval system without the written permission of the publisher except in the case of brief quotations embodied in critical articles and reviews.

ISBN 978-1-7033-8100-9

Fruit Salad Publishing
4308 Valencia Circle
Colorado Springs, CO 80917 USA

jeffboesel.com
prepareforimpact.life

CONTENTS

Prerequisite — 5

An Introduction and How to Use This Book — 9

1. Practical Preparation — 15
2. Spiritual Preparation — 21
3. Personal Preparation — 27
4. Culture Shock Preparation — 33
5. Emotional Preparation — 39
6. Security Preparation — 47
7. Educational Preparation — 55
8. Physical Preparation — 63
9. Experiential Preparation — 69
10. Cross–Cultural Preparation — 75
11. Financial Preparation — 83

Epilogue — 93

PREREQUISITE

I know what you are thinking: "There is a prerequisite for a book?" There is for this one! The prerequisite is the decision to get involved in cross-cultural work or ministry before reading this book! Though working abroad can be secular, kingdom-related, or both, I approach this topic from a ministry point of view. Many of the recommendations made, though, will assist anyone living and working cross-culturally.

Is this something God is asking you to do?

Often, we get involved in things that seem like the right thing to do for the wrong reasons. This isn't usually a huge deal, but when the decision requires you to completely uproot your life and the lives of others in your family, more consideration is needed. Let me share a couple of reasons that I feel are "wrong."

Sometimes we decide to pursue missions as part of an emotional response to a message or conference. It's not that God doesn't use these venues to lead someone into cross-cultural work. He does. But we need to make sure we are not guilted into it. A speaker relays the enormous need and implies that the only acceptable Christian response is to "go." The facts are undeniable. The lack is staggering. But guilt is never a reason to take on a new venture, especially a cross-cultural one!

Some get into missions because they grew up in a foreign culture and find it very difficult to fit back into their home culture. They can't speak English without an accent, nor can they relate to their home culture peer group's thinking. "Home" has become somewhere else, and they can't wait to get back there. Escapism is not a good foundation for a life of kingdom work.

In some churches, there is an unspoken belief that people in ministry have a closer walk with God. It is as if that vocation lifts them to a higher spiritual plane and that becoming a missionary is preferable to any secular job because it is wholly focused on kingdom growth. Let me be honest with you. Though at times we might have it all together, in reality, no one needs God's grace more than one of his missionaries!

Finally, some consider getting involved in cross-cultural work because they have lost their regular employment and, after trying to find a new job, feel that God must be leading them into a cross-cultural assignment. I have seen God use this technique with some people, most often when they have held onto their jobs as an idol and resisted obeying God's leading to get involved in kingdom work elsewhere (think Jonah). If this describes you, please obey and start looking for ways to get involved globally. But don't pursue missions only because you have lost a job and are struggling to find a new one.

These are only four of many unwise reasons for pursuing cross-cultural work. There is only one undeniable reason to pursue a cross-cultural kingdom commitment, and that is obedience to God's direct leading to do so.

If an act of obedience is where you find yourself, happy or angry, excited or dreadful, sure or doubtful, kicking and screaming or in full acceptance, please read on. I hope that this small book will be helpful to you along the way.

AN INTRODUCTION AND HOW TO USE THIS BOOK

Prepare for Impact is a guide for preparation in two ways. First, anyone going to live and work in another country should prepare for the impact that transition and cross-cultural living will have on them. Every culture is different, and the challenges faced may vary depending on the similarity to the new worker's home culture. Strangely, similar cultures are often more challenging to adapt to than ones that are significantly different. I attribute this to a blindside effect. When we transition somewhere similar to our home culture, from the United States to the United Kingdom, for example, we expect everything to be the same because so much is familiar. When we are confronted with the differences that exist, usually in an embarrassing way, we feel blindsided. But if the new culture is significantly different from our own, we expect everything to be different and anticipate that we will need to adapt. The stress then comes when those differences feel wrong in the face of our enculturation.

Second, anyone engaging another culture should prepare for the potential impact they will have on the people of that culture. Contrary to what we may want our impact to be, terms like "ugly American" have a basis in actual behavior. We act as if our beliefs and opinions are the correct ones and look down on others who hold different views. We may try to mold them into our cultural image instead of inspiring them to grow within their cultural norms. Maybe you have read the book *When Helping Hurts* by Steve Corbett and Brian Fikkert. If not, put it on your preparation book list. When we don't prepare to have a beneficial impact, the opposite is a distinct possibility and can create dependency. We can leave people in worse condition after helping than before we arrived.

It is possible to take adapting to another culture too far. Some expatriate people (expats) desire to "go native," thinking that is the best way to have an impact. This choice is not healthy. You will never completely transition into a person of another culture. Our best hope is to be a respected and significant outsider, or guest, of the host culture.

This book follows the misadventures of Sara Van Dussen, a fictional character who decides to go to a Latin American country for a yearlong missionary experience. Her college friend Meg is an employee of a mission agency who is serving long-term there. For some reason, Sara decides not to join an agency, but her heart is in the right place. Being born and raised in a Christ-following family in western Michigan gave her a solid foundation of faith. Attending Calvin College further solidified her commitment to Jesus and introduced her to the idea of being involved in advancing his kingdom. As time progressed, it became evident that God was leading her to spend her first year out of college in another country. She couldn't see much further than that. Maybe that is what kept her from joining an agency. Agencies wanted her to commit for two years, and that was just too long. In her last year at Calvin, she and Chad DeVries had started seriously dating, and being away from him for one year was going to be hard enough. Sara was sure God would not want her to serve him as a single missionary long-term. Maybe if Chad were not in her life, she would see that differently.

Instead of joining a mission agency, Sara had gone to the missions leadership of her church and asked if they would serve as her "sending agency." They had agreed, and between church, family, and friends she raised enough money to fund her year if she was careful with her spending. That would mean going without many things, including a cell phone and easy access to the Internet, but she was sure she could deal with that for one year. Sara had a plan to start a coffee ministry. It seemed like a given, living in a country where coffee was a major export and having been a barista for years. God had even provided extra funds to apply toward the start-up costs. She would turn the work over to some local church when it came time for her to leave. Much of this seemed impossible, but she believed she was serving God, and nothing is impossible for God.

Nearly all of Sara's adventures are based on real-life experiences lived by real-life missionaries who were not prepared for what they faced. In too many cases, that unprepared missionary was me!

So why listen to me? Since 2001, I have been helping people take steps toward impact on other cultures. It has become my passion and led me to create the organization Prepare for Impact. Over those years, I have become a student of what it takes to efficiently live and work in a cross-cultural setting. From 1993 to 2001, my family and I were missionaries in Guatemala, teaching other missionaries' children. In that role, I had the chance to experience living in another culture for myself and observe the lives of other workers there. In addition, my parents were also missionaries. They served in the Philippines, and I was with them there from age seven to eighteen. You might say living cross-culturally is part of the fabric of who I am. Even with these qualifications, I still recommend that you not take my word as absolute truth but rather as one person's take on practical preparation to serve and influence others.

Each chapter of this book contains a vignette from Sara's life, a related personal experience of mine, and some suggestions for preparation to help avoid, or at least lessen the impact of, that kind of event should you encounter it. Some things, like culture shock, are not avoidable. Other adverse experiences can be wholly sidestepped, as you will discover. Proper preparation will help you navigate your cross-cultural understanding with the best possible hopes for success.

This book is not meant to be an all-inclusive guide but more of a jumping-off point. As you consider the suggestions at the end of each chapter, they should lead you to initial actions and then hopefully guide you in your thinking to other things you could do. I don't want this to be overwhelming for you. Remember, you only need to take one step at a time. You will never be able to prepare for every possible challenge, but moving to another country without any real thought and action toward preparation could lead to disaster.

CHAPTER 1

PRACTICAL
PREPARATION

In which Sara finds that even simple things can be difficult

Sara stood outside the wrought iron gate and waved as Meg drove away in her BMW 2002, disappearing in a cloud of exhaust smoke. She wondered what her home church would think if they received an email asking for prayer because her "Beamer" was in the shop. She smiled, hoping Meg would make it back okay, but also somewhat proud that she had decided not to buy a vehicle. Public transport should be sufficient, right? She just needed to find a flat close enough to town that getting on a bus would be quick and easy–with a patio overlooking the city, and an extra bedroom for when her parents came to visit, and … She had to smile at herself as she realized how much like *House Hunters International* she sounded. *I wonder how one gets on that show,* she mused.

She laughed out loud and stepped back through the gate to the "welcoming committee"–Cassius and Brutus, Meg's two rottweilers, big, black, and slobbery. This pair was scary to look at but more of a danger to slime your new jeans than to hurt you. The locals didn't know that, though, and that was what mattered. Sara climbed up the concrete stairs to the second-floor bedroom she was using until she could find that perfect place of her own. Hearing her steps echo against the concrete walls and ceiling, she wondered why people didn't use more wood in construction. "It would be warmer," she thought, but then remembered that it was close to 100 degrees outside. "Cool is good," she said out loud.

Once in her room, she scooped up dirty clothes from her first week in the country and headed out the door. As she passed Meg's room, she noticed her laundry on the floor and thought she would help a little and add Meg's stuff to her own. She shook her head as she got to the kitchen, where the washing machine was located. "The washing machine in the kitchen?" she marveled. "Not in my apartment!" she said, doing her best *House Hunters International* imitation.

After throwing in the clothes and figuring out how to turn on the silly thing, she began to look for some detergent. *Hmmm, you'd think it would be right here.* Finally, she found a single-use box; at least, that is what it looked like. She couldn't understand the container's Spanish label, but it showed a person pouring it into a washing machine on the side. *Tinta* didn't sound like "soap" or "detergent," but she didn't think anything she heard in Spanish sounded like the English word it was supposed to represent. She shrugged, opened the box, and poured it into the already agitating water.

The instant the powder hit the water, it changed from its lily-white color to a purplish-black–and so did the water, and so did the clothes closest to the surface of the water. Sara gasped. All she could get to come out of her mouth was "Oh-oh-oh-oh!" She grabbed an armful of wet and darkening clothes out of the washer and looked around for what to do. She headed toward the open bathroom door down the hall, trailing the darkly dyed water behind her. She jumped into the shower, still holding the clothes in her hands, and turned on the water. Now soaked from head to toe, she headed back to the machine, still running and now filled with completely black water. She shoved the "start" dial in to stop the machine and scooped the rest of the clothes out, now praying, "Please no, please no, please no" as she headed back to the bathroom. The clothes she had left there had regained some of their original colors, but she sadly realized that she had ruined the entire load. She dropped to her knees in the shower, tears joining with the cool water pouring over her, but they served to lighten neither the clothes nor her spirit. What would Meg say?

All of Sara's chronicles are based on true stories that happened to real people just trying to have an impact for the kingdom. A little practical preparation in language learning may have saved Sara from the embarrassing and costly mistake of adding dye to her load of laundry. In time, she and Meg were able to laugh about it, and they had a great time shopping for new clothes together that weekend.

My wife and I remember standing in front of a Burger King in Guatemala and tearing up because we didn't even know whether we were supposed to pull or push the doors to get in. One side said *Hale* while the other said *Empuje*. Of course we could figure it out by trial and error, but that wasn't the point. The point was that we were beginning to learn Spanish and didn't know what a preschooler would know, even while holding university degrees and having more than twenty years' experience in the education and business world.

Maybe because preparation along practical lines seems obvious, it is often overlooked. As you consider what practical preparation to undertake, make sure you add the following to your list:

1. Ensure that the leadership of your home church knows of your consideration of these steps. Fortunately for Sara, she had done this as part of her preparation process, so she had a family of God's people praying for her regularly. Your sending church can be your most significant support and guide on this journey and may even have a preparation process for missionaries they support. There is probably no better training than that. You will be an extension of their ministry wherever you go, which is your best-case scenario.

2. Declutter. Many of us, especially in the United States, have way more stuff than we need. When we first went to Guatemala, we stored many things in our house's attic and the barn of a supporter friend. Some of it was sentimental stuff we still have, but we gave the rest of it away when we got back. Why didn't we do that initially? Shrink your physical footprint.

3. Learn to live more simply. Missionary work is not the career you should be pursuing if you want to be comfortable by US standards. Most agencies try to provide funding adequate for living at a middle-class level for the area you are in; however, that may be well below your current standard of living. Our "extravagance" can be a deterrent to our witness, even though we wouldn't consider it extravagance in our own culture. I am not recommending that you try to "become" a national. You can't. As a Guatemalan friend once told us, "Your mother's not Guatemalan." Strive to be an accepted and respected outsider to the culture.

4. If you have a sense of where God is leading you, begin to acclimate yourself to culture and language by developing relationships with people of that culture within your local area. Research may be required, but that too is good preparation for what is ahead. There is value in language learning programs, but I would more strongly recommend a relational learning approach or a combination of the two. Learning vocabulary and grammar is only learning the face of a language. Understanding how words and grammar are used in a given situation is getting to the heart of a language. Being tutored online by a native speaker of your target language is being used by many. Proper language learning cannot happen apart from cultural knowledge.

5. If you are a meat-and-potatoes kind of person, you might want to consider expanding your palate now. Most cities in the United States have a selection of ethnically based restaurants from which to choose. In many cultures, it isn't very respectful to the host if you do not eat the food placed in front of you, whatever it is. If this is scary, ask longer-term expats in the country if there are gracious ways of excusing yourself from eating what is offered.

6. Depending on where you are going, if you know the location, get an "International Driving Permit." You can apply for one from AAA. It isn't a legal license, but it serves to translate your US license into most major languages. You might be surprised how often having one can help. At some point, you may want to go through the process of applying for a local license. Sara did. You'll find out what happened in chapter 3!

7. Make out a will. You may not have a lot, or anything, to leave behind if you die, but this is still essential. Your wishes, should you die, may not be very important to you, but they are to your family, and that includes your agency.

Practical preparation is one of the most logical areas to see what could and should be done. None of the things I recommend here are expensive financially, but they will cost you some time and energy. Not all of them will be comfortable for you, but neither will living in another country!

CHAPTER 2

SPIRITUAL PREPARATION

In which Sara finds a new reason for going to church

Sara hit the snooze on her alarm yet again, but although generally awake, she lay in bed struggling with why she didn't want to get up. It was Sunday morning, and she knew she should be getting ready to go to church. She had rarely dealt with such a negative feeling about church. Was it that different here? She forced herself to a sitting position. Her headache from living in Spanish was numbing her senses; well, all except her sense of smell, now attacked by the ever-so-familiar odor of diesel fumes from the bus stop right below her flat.

She picked up her still-damp towel and walked into the bathroom to see if a shower would change her attitude and clear her head. After turning on the water, she flipped on the switch for the "widow-maker."* Standing there watching the

---

* Widow-maker is a term given to a type of water heater mounted on the showerhead which circulates water through an electric coil to heat it. A short in the coil can bring about quite a shock for the person in the shower, as you might imagine!

water flow drop to little more than a trickle, she wondered about the chances of electrocution at the hands of such a device. She finally shrugged and stepped into the mostly warm water. *Not today, I guess,* she mused.

Late again, she thought as she picked her way through the maze of people in the aisle of the bus, trying to escape before the driver, anxious for the next possible fare, picked up too much speed for a safe jump. She was glad she hadn't worn heels. She weaved her way across the street, directing traffic with her hands in hopes of making it to the church building in one piece. Slipping into the service without being noticed was never an option here. First, the elders were standing just inside the door, greeting people as they arrived and taking note of who did not. Next, being the only tall, blonde, white woman in the building was an issue. It was as if the room actually got brighter as she walked in because everyone seemed to know, turn toward her, and greet her verbally! She slipped into a seat near the back and tried to focus.

The singing had started. It was a hymn Sara knew, but what were the words in English? She stood there a moment, totally frustrated. "I can't sing this in English or Spanish," she said audibly. The lady next to her looked, smiled, and went on singing. Sara forced a smile back and hummed. When the pastor stepped up to speak, Sara pulled out her notepad, though she wasn't going to take notes on the message. She was planning to record the words she recognized. Hopefully, there would be more than last week. Did this guy know any verbal speed other than light speed?

Sara had discovered that maintaining your spiritual life can get a little complicated in a new and different culture. Some places are easier than others or have more resources for English speakers, like English-speaking churches, but that is certainly not the case in more remote locations. Developing healthy spiritual rhythms before you arrive in your adopted country is critical to your continued spiritual growth, even your spiritual survival.

The last year in the US before we left for Guatemala was probably the most spiritually significant year of my life. It seemed that God was doing miraculous things each day. I heard the leading of his Spirit spoken directly into my brain. As I excitedly shared this with my father, a veteran missionary of thirty-plus years at that time, he mused, "You may find that changes when you get to Guatemala." That took me off guard, and so, like all the other times I get taken off guard, I shrugged and figured my dad was speaking for himself and couldn't possibly understand the tight relationship God and I had. How wrong I was!

About six months into our time in Guatemala, Dad's words echoed in my brain. I found myself in some "magical box" that held all my prayers in and kept all of God's voice out. I wanted to say, "My God, my God, why have you forsaken me?" but I knew that was stupid. Jesus had taken that fall and opened the way, so that would never be true for me. He had promised never to leave me. So where was he, or better yet, where was I?

I know of many stories where a missionary left for another country feeling that they were fully equipped spiritually, only to find that failure in their spiritual lives made them ineffective or ended their missionary career. Don't ignore the following in your spiritual preparation.

1. Develop habits of feeding yourself spiritually. If you end up in a place where English is not the commonly spoken tongue, you may have little opportunity to worship in your language, making self-led growth critical. Depending on the difficulty of the host country's language, it could be years before you feel that going to church is helping you move forward in your spiritual walk. Remember also that language is just one issue of difference in a new culture.

   What would this kind of self-feeding include? As with spiritual growth in your home culture, spending regular time focused on your relationship with God is vital. Any relationship you truly value requires time, energy, and sacrifice. Your relationship with God is no different. Communication and communion with him, along with being immersed in his Word, are essential. Surrounding yourself with people also growing in him is helpful, and though a little more difficult in a cross-cultural setting, not impossible. You must understand and accept that the time needed for this deepening of your walk with God will require sacrificing time of doing ministry outwardly. Don't minimize the importance of spiritual self-care in ministry.

2. Declutter your spiritual life. In our home culture, we hold onto bad habits that may have a cultural background, like our egocentric individualism in the United States. We may also have issues rooted in our basic sin nature, like a bent toward angry outbursts. These are habits we know are wrong, deep down, but that we justify somehow. Because we are "at home," we can keep them safely hidden and mostly under control. It is best to deal with these before you find yourself in another culture rather than deal with them amid cross-cultural stress. Cross-cultural living tends to bring out the evils we thought were defeated, or at least under control.

   It is best to talk to important people in your life whom you trust and to whom you will listen when decluttering like this. Permit them to be honest with you about unhealthy things they see in you. Ask them to hold you accountable to make the necessary changes. Talk to missionaries you know about what things they saw in their lives as they began to live and work in another country or culture. Look for similar issues in your own life and take steps to address them.

3. Deepen your prayer life. As with the above, we often get by with a minimal amount of time spent in prayer in our US-based Christianity. We find we can do most things on our own. What is even more difficult for us is that we value this highly in our culture. Independence is next to godliness! Actually, of course, the opposite is true.

Dependence is the only way forward spiritually. Trust me; nothing will bring you to dependence quicker than cross-cultural living. You are not in Kansas anymore, Dorothy! Begin now making prayer the priority of your spiritual walk.

4. **Develop the profound skill of listening to God.** Most of us are too busy to take time to listen in prayer. Our time with God is usually consumed in the "ask" mode. The tendency toward asking will intensify under cross-cultural stress. The spiritual battle becomes more real. People get spiritually injured. There is urgency. Start now forcing yourself to spend time quietly before God, listening for his voice through the din. He promised us that we would recognize it as his sheep, but we have to be quiet enough to hear it! This is also a critical spiritual discipline for fund development.

    How do you start? Start small. During your regular prayer time, set aside one minute to be still and quiet and listen. If you have not done this before, you will be surprised at how long one minute is! If you need to, start with thirty seconds. Wherever you start, slowly increase the amount of time you spend listening until it equals or surpasses the amount of time you spend asking.

Whereas the practical preparation we considered in the previous chapter is the most logical, spiritual preparation is probably the most needed, especially if you will be directly involved with kingdom work. Make your spiritual preparation a high priority!

CHAPTER 3

PERSONAL PREPARATION

In which Sara finds that getting a driver's license requires more than driving

Sara stood transfixed in the doorway of a smallish room crammed full of humanity. Her mouth was open so wide that one of the local buses could have driven into it. It wasn't the crowded conditions that held her gaze, nor was it the usual heat combined with the typical smell. What stopped her in her tracks that morning was her unrestricted view into the men's restroom with men using the facilities in the sight of God and everyone else!

Before she had a chance to process this information and form a guess as to what was happening, she was shoved into the waiting room by those behind her who were eager to spend the rest of their day waiting in line. Trying to keep her eyes averted from the "scenery," she set about her task of figuring out the process for obtaining a driver's license. She glanced at the scribbled list given to her by Meg and found the line extending from the desk where the process would begin. She had become pretty good at securing her place in a line here, and she certainly needed that skill at this moment. She braced herself, physically and mentally, for the wait.

Realizing she was in for a long day, she thankfully, and somewhat proudly, reflected on having the foresight to use "the facilities" at her flat before leaving for this Latin American version of a DMV. She mentally reviewed what she had studied in preparation for the driving test. In what seemed a very short time, she found herself jostled to the front of the line and facing a young clerk who handed her a form and a lidded plastic cup. Her puzzled look brought on some Spanish spoken way too quickly for her to understand and an arm pointing toward the ladies' room. Was a urine sample required for a driver's license? The open men's room door was now beginning to make sense. With a spike of panic, she shot a glance at the ladies' room and, to her relief, found the door to be closed.

Her relief was short-lived, though, as she realized she had an empty bladder. Why, of all mornings, had she chosen this morning to prepare for a long day without visiting a restroom? Sara sighed and leaned against a nearby wall. She opened her water bottle and started to drink. At least she hadn't left home without that!

An hour passed and she finally made her way into the restroom. The open men's room door was just to her left as she entered, and she was glad once again for some semblance of modesty and privacy. She completed her task and tried not to look embarrassed as she took the sample to desk number two. The line was short, thankfully. She handed her specimen to the lady behind the desk, who shook her head and handed it right back with one word: "*Mas!*" But Sara didn't possess any "more" to give. She tried to make a case for her plight in her best broken Spanish, but the result was another arm pointing toward the restroom door.

Standing once again in a restroom stall (sitting was not an option due to the usual lack of a toilet seat), Sara wondered what to do. She was out of water, in all ways that mattered, but she still needed to produce some if she was going to get her license without having to start over. As she stood there perplexed, someone at the sink outside her stall cleared her throat. Sara had an idea. Urine was not the only bodily fluid she had at her disposal. She held the cup not too close to her mouth and began to spit into it.

A little while later as she walked out of the office holding her temporary license, she smiled, shook her head, and wondered how she would fit that story into her next blog post.

Though it took her a while, Sara was able to find a solution to her problem without leaving to try again another day. Adaptability is an essential skill, both before and after you arrive in a different country.

Our personal experience was not as pretty as Sara's. It happened within our first couple of months in Guatemala. Learning to drive safely there was a lesson in patience, flexibility, and faith. One day we got lost, and in trying to get back to a place we knew, we went down a one-way street the wrong way. There were no signs and no other cars visible, but when we got to the end of the road, a police officer was there to stop us. In a panic, I ended up giving him the equivalent of about fifty dollars to get out of there. Once we got back to our office, I told my team leader what had happened. He drove us back to that same intersection and talked it out with the officer, and, in the end, we got our money back. Though we were thankful for the money's return, the experience left us feeling thoroughly embarrassed and unprepared to be living and driving in that city.

Some people are just more flexible and adaptable than others, but that doesn't mean we can't learn to be more flexible than we naturally are in our own culture. Here are some suggestions to help you move forward in this area.

1. Take one or two **personality assessments** to discover your natural bent toward challenging situations. Myers–Briggs and the Enneagram are good choices, but you might also consider others. CliftonStrengths (formerly Clifton StrengthsFinder by Gallup) helps you understand what skills may empower you. The DiSC assessment enables you to know what you contribute to a team trying to accomplish a task. There are other assessments, but these are widely known and easy to find. To gain the most significant benefit from these assessments, plan to meet with someone who has expertise in evaluating them. The agency you join may also help you.

2. Schedule a meeting with a counselor to help you think through how you react in difficult situations. Counseling is a great resource when taking steps toward a significant cross-cultural transition. Whether dealing with brokenness in your past or relationships in your present, speaking with a counselor can help you identify the root areas to address to become more emotionally healthy.

3. Talk to friends and family about how they see you. You may think you are flexible and adapt well to new situations, but others may not see that in you. This may be one of the most challenging things to do, because some of their feedback may be hard to hear; however, if we are to grow, facing ourselves as we are and as others experience us is necessary. Your family and good friends love you. Better to hear hard things from them than from people you don't know.

4. Take on some new and challenging things that will force you to think on your feet and adapt to changing situations. Your own culture is the best place to begin a process of growing in adaptability and resilience. Getting outside of your areas of comfort will stretch you and broaden your base of experiences. When you go to live in another culture, everything is likely to be different–having been in new situations before that significant change will pay dividends.

5. **Watch others** who seem to handle challenges well. Take notes and then sit down with them and talk about how they do it. If you can learn from others' experiences, you will be way better off in the long run. You cannot discover everything this way, because some things are best understood by experiencing them. However, you may be able to avoid many heartaches if you can personalize the lessons learned by others who have gone before you. One of the most important skills you can teach yourself before leaving is to observe and then apply what you know.

If God is leading you on a path toward cross-cultural living, you will experience personal growth. Situating yourself to make the most of those growth opportunities is like repotting a plant in good soil. In the transition process, the plant encounters significant stress, but if the receiving soil is good, it will overcome the stress and become even stronger than it was before. You want to live that way!

CHAPTER 4

CULTURE SHOCK
PREPARATION

In which Sara finds that living in another culture brings out your crazy

It was one of those experiences where you feel like you are separated from your body, watching as you act in a way you never thought possible. In horror and disbelief, Sara gazed at herself standing in the middle of the volleyball court, screaming at the top of her lungs before stomping off. She plopped herself into the driver's seat of Meg's BMW. "Crap!" Those black vinyl seats were hot! She picked up the bottle of way-too-warm water next to her. It felt hot enough to brew tea, if only she had some. As she worked to twist the top off the bottle, it slipped in her sweaty hands and spilled all over her lap. "Crap!" she said again, though other words fought for dominance in her brain. What was happening? Why was she so angry all of a sudden? Was this really her?

As she tried to regroup in the car, she forced herself to look out at the game still in progress. Whatever confusion she had caused by her meltdown had vanished, and her potential friends, though it may be a distant possibility to call them that now, were laughing, arguing, cheering, swearing, and generally just having a great time over beer, wine, and volleyball. Well, that is what they called the game, but they were playing it all wrong. She turned the key, and the car rumbled to life. Flipping on the air conditioning, she let her head drop back against the ripped headrest and closed her eyes.

Just a few short months ago, Sara had been peering out the window of a Boeing 737 as it carried her over the capital city on the approach to its international airport. *I'm finally here,* she had thought, *where God can use me to show his love for these people.* She was quite sure at that point that she didn't need the wings of the aircraft to be flying. The strength of her resolve and her joy and excitement would easily keep her feet off the ground. Her first weeks had been a flurry of excitement and discovery. This was it! She was in the right place at the right time for the right reason. What had happened between then and now? She just couldn't put her finger on it.

A loud rapping on the window jump-started her brain back to the present. It took a second or two to reorient herself in space and time. She realized she had been crying. Wiping the tear tracks from her cheeks, she sheepishly smiled at Luz, one of her volleyball friends, and rolled down the window. "Sara," Luz said in a friendly but scolding voice, *"no safe be aquí, sola."* Luz was quite proud of her Spanglish, and it showed. Sara tried to blurt out a thank-you and an apology at the same time, but Luz wagged her finger as she bounded away toward her vehicle. *"No tengas pena!"* she called back over her shoulder. *"Hasta la próxima–ciao!"*

Our missionary is deep into cross-cultural adjustment. The stress of living in her adopted culture has caused Sara to think and act somewhat irrationally. Though cross-cultural stress affects people in different ways, nearly everyone who has experienced it would agree that it tends to bring out the worst in us. Often, we find out things about ourselves that we never knew existed.

My personal story would have me standing at the front door of our house in Guatemala, screaming at the top of my lungs. I was imploring my family to get in the car and wondering how much damage would be done if I tried to put my fist through the hallway's concrete block wall. We would be late again. Some of you may be saying, "What is so abnormal about that?" On the rational side, we were going to be late for church yet again, and besides being personally embarrassing it might not reflect well on us as missionaries to the church in that country. On the irrational side, we were going to a Guatemalan church where the pastor didn't always arrive "on time," and some members would walk in for the last five minutes of the service!

I often describe living in another culture in terms of an irritation that isn't bad enough to make you leave but always exists. It is like a persistent dull headache. You learn to live with it, but it impacts everything you do. For Sara, the irritant was a volleyball game, a game she recognized because everything about it appeared to be the same as in her home country–the court, the ball, and the net. However, the way the game was played in her new country was different, and she had no clue what those differences were. Even after learning the local strategy, deep in her heart she had the conviction that the game was being misplayed.

Unfortunately, for those of us whom God has directed to live in another culture, there is no real preparation strategy to shield us from the effects of "culture shock." It is possible, though, to minimize its impact by following a few simple steps.

1. **Do some research.** Do lots of research. The Internet is a wonderful thing, and it can help you begin a foundation upon which to build your future cross–cultural life, even before you step onto the airport jet bridge. Become a student of your target culture and learn everything you can about it.

2. If possible, **search out communities near you that come from the culture you will be entering.** The world is literally in our backyard. Once you find pockets of your target culture, find ways to engage them. "Too hard," you say. If you think this is too hard, maybe you should rethink your belief that God wants you to leave home to relocate to that culture. If you can't engage them in your culture, you will struggle to engage them in their culture. Finding a local church that ethnicity attends is an easier option than trying to crash a backyard party you happen to come across on a walk around the neighborhood! Ethnic restaurants and grocery stores are also helpful starting places.

3. **Invest in a language learning program or a native speaking tutor** to give you a foundation for learning the language. A large part of the stress of being in another culture is not understanding what is going on around you. Looking back at Sara in her volleyball game, she didn't understand what was said around her. When people laughed, she wondered, *Are they laughing at me?* You get the idea. With all the available resources, there is no reason not to have at least a basic grasp of the target language vocabulary.

4. **Plan a trip to that country** to visit before moving there to stay for a longer time. This is expensive, yes, but it will pay off in the time it can save you adjusting after settling in. If you have already been there, save your money and put your time, energy, and money toward other preparation needs.

Culture shock can be crushing. I have seen many leave their country of service prematurely as a result of that one thing. Others may not have left, but scars from the initial cross-cultural stress impacted their life and ministry afterward. Some ended up in relationships that were not healthy. This even happens to Sara, but that story is still ahead. Do everything you can now to lessen the impact of a new culture on your life.

CHAPTER 5

EMOTIONAL
PREPARATION

In which Sara finds that distance sometimes leads to disaster

Sara peered at the fingerprint-smudged screen in the dimly lit, smoke-filled cybercafe. The hardly discernible hourglass cursor was still flip-flopping as her email home page attempted to load. She thought seriously about clicking on the "Load the simple HTML version" link, but she knew that would slide her back to square one in this frustrating Chutes-and-Ladders nightmare. She reached for her coffee cup and raised it to her lips. Just then, a careless bump to the back of her head from someone behind her sent lukewarm coffee cascading down the front of her blouse. *"Personal space!"* her mind screamed so loud that she was sure those close to her could hear it.

Sara examined the brown stain, now the prominent feature of her blouse, wondering if the local coffee was better at staining clothing than it was at tasting good. Apparently, all the decent product was exported from this coffee-growing country, leaving the locals to brew the sweepings from the coffee bean drying floors. Where is a Starbucks when you really need it?

The change in brightness of the screen drew her attention back to it. Seventeen new messages! Her heart jumped with anticipation though her mind fought to control the excitement, reminding her that junk mail was a respecter of neither location nor sacrifice. Sara opened her inbox and scanned the subject lines. There were three from her mom, one from her bank, a boatload of junk, and one from Chad! An excited schoolgirl "yes!" escaped her lips, which drew the nearby Internet junkies' momentary attention. Still, within seconds, everyone appeared buried once again within the glow of their habit.

Deciding to leave Chad for "dessert," she made quick work of deleting the junk mail–a little too quick, as the email from her bank disappeared from the page. Sara sighed and clicked on the deleted mail folder to retrieve it. Opening the file, she scanned the message, which had something to do with her school loans. Too much brainpower was needed for this one so early in the morning. She clicked "forward" and typed in her dad's address and one word: "Help?!" Dad would know what to do with it, and it would give him an excuse to write her, as he never seemed to do so without one! She smiled but then realized how much that sounded like something her mom would say. The smile vanished. She loved her parents, but the idea of becoming them was not wholly appealing!

It was always good to hear from her mom, but those emails were never quickly handled. She fought the temptation to give lip service to what she knew her mom wanted to hear. *No, Mom would see right through that and begin wondering what was going on.* Then, a video chat was sure to follow, which wouldn't be a horrible thing, she mused. Though it would be awkward, if not impossible, in this kind of a place. Maybe she could jack Meg's Internet connection for that. What was taking the phone company so long to get her landline in anyway? It had been over a month since she placed the order. She was pretty sure she had done that right. Maybe she should make sure that something wasn't .... What was she doing? Chad was waiting!

Sara had met Chad their junior year at Calvin, and they had been on the path toward a life together since then. No confirming "question" had been popped, but it was a done deal in her mind. Chad was the guy God intended for her. Then unexpectedly, God opened this door to a one-year missionary experience beginning just after graduation. The only thing Sara was more certain of than being with Chad was that God wanted her here, now. It was confusing, but that seemed to be God's MO in dealing with her. She knew him well enough to recognize his fingerprints. Anyway, it was just a year, right?

The message filled the screen, and the immediate oddity was how short it was. Sara's brow furrowed. Her eyes dropped quickly to the end of the note, where she always began, and all she found there was a very unemotional "Chad." She leaned in toward the screen, instinctively feeling that would make her experience more private in such an unprivate place, and began to read. She bit her lip. Her eyes flooded. "Why, God?" she whispered. She closed her eyes, and tears, dropping to her blouse, began to lighten the coffee stain. She was thankful for the dimness of the room and an inattentive audience. Her fingers started moving across the keyboard instinctively.

"Dear Mom …," she began.

What could be taking the phone company so long?

The breakup that Sara is about to experience happens to many singles in serious relationships over long separations. What makes Sara's situation a little more challenging is that this comes on top of the many other difficulties she faces living and working in a culture different from how she was raised.

My wife, Deänne, is the director of MemberCare for our agency. In my conversations with her and from interactions with other caregivers at worldwide conferences, I can safely say that emotional issues are a huge concern within missions projects. Harry Hoffman, the coordinator for the Global Member Care Network, describes support for an individual in terms of several pillars that provide balance and stability. When we move from our current locale to somewhere new, we eliminate many of those pillars, and they must be reestablished in our new location to achieve balance again. A list of all contributing "pillars" would certainly range beyond preparation alone. Still, some attention to emotional preparation for such a transition and the anticipated increase in stress is undoubtedly needed.

Emotional health is essential to effective impact in another culture. Please consider the following in thinking through emotional preparation:

1. Cross–cultural ministry often requires a lot of leaving, and leaving can be done well or, if not an item of focus,

poorly. There has been much research done on this. I would recommend the process developed by the late David Pollock called Building Your Raft presented in the book entitled *Third Culture Kids* by David Pollock, Ruth Van Reken, and Michael Pollock (© 2009 Nicholas Brealey Publishing, Third Edition). I have summarized it here.

Reconciliation: Make sure you take time to deal with any negative issues you have with those you are connected to, both near and far. Examples of these issues may be unresolved conflict, emotional hurt, bitterness, and harbored anger or resentment. The emotional fractures created by concerns like these tend to grow larger when exposed to the stress of living in another culture.

Affirmation: Make sure that you also liberally hand out thanksgiving to those who have contributed to your life. You do not know what God's plans are for you or them. This may be your last chance to tell them how much they mean to you.

Farewells: Make sure you take the time to say goodbye to people, places, and things you will be leaving behind. I am sure saying goodbye to people makes sense to most of us, but places and things also hold importance in our hearts and minds. I made the choice to leave our two dogs behind in Guatemala when we returned to the United States. I am not sure my family has let me off the hook for that decision yet!

Think destination: Make sure you take considerable time to think about what is ahead. Talk to those who are there or have been there. Allow anticipation to build for the new things that new location will bring to you. Get excited.

Remembering these four things is easiest using the acronym RAFT. Ensure that, if you have children coming with you, they do all these things as well. If they are adults and are not coming with you, make sure they get to spend some time with you in your new location. Many adult children consider home to be where their parents live. Your move just made that a different place, and it will be vital for them to have a connection there.

2. As mentioned in the chapter on personal preparation, consider getting some counseling to help you walk through your life and deal with any issues hanging on from past hurts. This advice would be in addition to the "reconciliation" piece of RAFT described above. The counseling may help you identify relationships you need to address in RAFT. I am not recommending counseling because you need significant outside help with a specific issue. Sometimes we are blind to the things that roadblock us because we are too close to them, and an outside person (especially a trained one) can help us see more clearly. Remember, cross–cultural stress tends to bring out our ugliness. Don't go into it with more "baggage" than you must.

3. If you are married, consider doing some marriage counseling. Again, this is not to imply that you need it in your own culture, but living cross-culturally tends to strip us bare of all the coping habits we have developed to "deal" with that person living with us. We all have those, so it may be useful to understand them before you go. Also, healthy communication between you and your spouse is critical, and a counselor may help you improve that part of your relationship. Often in cross-cultural ministry settings, your spouse becomes your venting place because they are "safe." You can't vent to your colleagues or the people you are ministering to, and you want to be careful not to take your frustration out on your children if you have them. Your spouse is available and close, and your relationship has a private element. When this happens, and there are other, deeper personal issues, those venting times can go way beyond venting.

4. Don't transition while in the middle of potential life-changing relationships. This is what tripped up Sara. It may have been best for her to "play out" her relationship with Chad before her departure date, or at least have a significant discussion with him about the separation and the possible outcomes. Her assumption that all would remain as it was when she left was just not realistic. Nothing remains static.

Emotional preparation is difficult because we rarely want to admit weakness in that area of our lives. Perhaps in your own culture, with all your supporting structures, you are getting along just fine. However, brokenness is real for most of us, and when we get into situations of extreme stress, those cracks become visible. Please don't sell yourself short when it comes to taking the steps necessary to prepare yourself emotionally.

CHAPTER 6

SECURITY
PREPARATION

*In which Sara finds that mustard is
more than just a condiment*

The large sliding-glass doors automatically parted as Sara approached them, and artificially cooled air washed over her. The unmistakable smell of a big-box store filled her nostrils, and her eyes took in what seemed to be an endless number of checkout stations. She would have thought she had stepped into a different time and place except for the jostling of darker-colored skin all around her and the ever-present sound of Spanish, which she was growing to love as a way of expression. *I suppose I could be in Miami,* she mused with a smile, remembering a local joke about how much Latinos like Miami. "It's so close to the United States," they would say.

That mass of humanity, full of excitement, forced her forward into the store. It was opening day at PriceSmart, and everyone wanted to be there to experience what was indeed a feast for the senses. Row after row of tall metal scaffolding stood proudly upon shiny porcelain tile floors, rising to yet-higher ceilings decorated with an intentional pattern of exposed air conditioning pipes, electrical conduits, and hundreds of fluorescent light fixtures. The scaffolding supported boxes upon boxes of attractively packaged products just waiting to be placed into a cart, wheeled to one of the forty checkout lines, and purchased. There was even a café with brats, pizza, soda, and ice cream. Sarah suddenly felt hungry but pushed that urge aside as she examined the line of people who had the same feeling, extending on to forever. She wondered if the water they used in the sodas and ice was *"agua pura."* Maybe, maybe not. *Did it really matter?* she wondered.

Sara allowed herself to get lost in the overwhelming experience. She walked up and down the aisles, which were teeming with people, recognizing this product and that, most of which she had not seen in the last several months of living here. No cart inhibited her progress because she had no money, to speak of, to spend. She hadn't come to buy anything anyway. It was the anticipated experience that had drawn her; the experience of being home.

Suddenly she became aware of the strong scent of mustard. *Strange,* she thought as she looked around for a sample stand with an open jar of mustard. Seeing none, she shrugged and was about to move on when a young couple approached her with apologetic, if not somewhat shocked, looks on their faces. With a flurry of apologies, they directed her eyes to lines of mustard decorating the back and shoulders of her shirt. *Crap!* she thought. I just got the coffee stain out of the front of this! Her mind wandered for a split second to Chad, and her eyes threatened to tear up, but she forced herself back to the present with a shake of her head. The young couple was offering to help, and in fact, were already helping by wiping up the mustard with paper towels. Between the masses of onlookers, her attempt to understand what was being said, and the overwhelming attention to her plight, she felt a moment of panic. She forced herself to take a mental breath and collect herself.

The mustard that had not become part of her shirt was now smeared on paper towels and thrown away, and she found herself thanking her "good Samaritans" over and over for their help. They smiled, apologized once again for the embarrassing experience she had just suffered while in their country, and then turned and left as suddenly as they had appeared.

Sara let out a long sigh, deciding that this experience should come to an end soon. On her way to the exit, she passed the book section, marveling that nearly all of them were in English. Near the end of the row, Sara noticed a parallel version of the Bible in English and Spanish, something she had been trying to find ever since her arrival. She picked it up and headed for the checkout, thankful she hadn't come entirely devoid of money. The wait in line was long, but she passed the time thumbing through the Bible, looking at familiar passages to see how they would read in Spanish. Finally reaching the register, she watched the price flash onto the LCD screen and reached for her wallet. Not finding it immediately, she dug deeper into her bag–still nothing. "I know I brought it," she assured herself, looking down into the gaping mouth of her purse. Her eyes fell on a mustard stain.

This didn't feel like home anymore.

In this experience, Sara allowed herself to become so overwhelmed and distracted by the newness and excitement of what was going on around her that she became blind to other, very real, things that were happening. In the area of security, this is the biggest threat. When we first arrive in a new place that carries some risk (theft fueled by poverty, fundamentalist religious violence, etc.), we usually are on our guard against potential threats. However, after living in a place for a while, things eventually seem normal, and we sometimes forget to be aware of what is happening around us. Brand-new experiences, like the one Sara had, also can throw us off our normal sensitivity. The new store felt so much like home, but in reality, risks were still there.

Our most scary experience involved being held at gunpoint while in a remote location on top of an active volcano. Just rereading that sentence makes me wonder why we thought it was okay to do. We had done some research before going, and many others had done the same hike with no problems. We took no money or valuables. We were in a group of sixteen, seven of whom were adults. But guns and explosive devices are great equalizers in terms of numbers. Some terrible things happened during that experience, but we all returned alive, which was a victory. Many in those kinds of situations today do not turn out as well.

I don't mention these things to try to convince you not to go. If God leads you to go somewhere, you need to respond in obedience no matter the risk. When you go, I hope you will prepare yourself in such a way that you will not become complacent and caught unaware. Please consider the following as you prepare to move to a new, possibly less secure, culture.

1. Nearly every agency will require require a background check on you, which is not a big deal unless you have a police record of some kind. This usually doesn't end your hopes of being a missionary, but it may limit where you can get a visa.

2. Contact the State Department, or at least go to their website, and discover what your government says about visiting or living in the country you are considering. Again, this is not to say that you allow what you find out to cause you to bail out (obedience, remember?), but it will give you one view of the place you are going.

3. Make sure you check in with the US Embassy soon after arrival and register that you live there, giving them your contact information. This is critically important. If an evacuation should become necessary, they can only make sure you are out of the country if they know you are there and how to reach you.

4. Talk to people in your organization, or others you know, who live and work in that country and city. They will bring a helpful balance to what you hear from the government about what to expect. Research is your friend. The more you know, the better prepared you will be.

5. Learn and practice countersurveillance. This is relatively easy and is something you should practice even in your home culture. As you prepare to leave any location, be aware of the new "environment" you are about to enter. What and where are the potential dangers? If people are visible, make eye contact with them, even greet them. If a potential assailant knows that you have already recognized them, they will most likely look for an easier target. Get in the habit of playing the "what if?" game. For example, when you leave the grocery store, imagine where you would go and what you would do if you were confronted dangerously. The most important underlying principle is this: **do not be caught unaware.**

6. Ensure that your family knows a **code phrase** you would use in a message to them if you were kidnapped. That will assure your family that you are indeed still alive. I know that sounds scary, but the fact is people do get kidnapped and held for ransom in many countries around the world. Make sure you regularly review your agency policy on kidnapping and other crises. No matter where you go, you should have an exit strategy that you review periodically. In some places, you will want to have a "go bag" always ready.

7. Practice not making yourself a potential target. In addition to the above, plan to not draw attention to yourself. Don't wear things that appear expensive or

that you cannot afford to lose (like expensive jewelry). If you purchase a car, choose one that is not highly valued and often stolen. Carry just the amount of money you need for the specific purpose of your outing. Never flash it around. Women, keep your purse under your arm or in your lap. Men, consider carrying your wallet in your front pocket. Be careful with credit cards. Be very familiar with your card company's policy on fraudulent charges. Use common sense.

8. Have certified/legalized copies of all your essential documents made in your host country. They may need to be translated and stamped by an authorizing office to be acceptable if you are asked for them. Passports, visas, and other identifying documents should be kept in a safe or other secure location. Your agency may require that the originals be kept at their office if they have one.

Much more can be said about security, but this will get you started. Though you may think bad things won't happen to you, know that others had that same thought just before something happened to them. On the other hand, I am not recommending that you live in fear. There is a balance between being prepared and being obsessed. Work to find that healthy balance.

CHAPTER 7

EDUCATIONAL PREPARATION

In which Sara finds that God gives Christmas presents

Sara lay in bed, her eyes glazed and staring at the stucco ceiling while her ears were bombarded with the constant sound of fireworks exploding all around her. Occasional flashes of light from the explosions filled her room through the window that allowed both light and diesel fumes to enter. *"Do these people ever go to sleep?"* she thought as she forced her eyes closed. Some of her expat friends had told her this night would be "exciting." But she had not anticipated this level of excitement. She suspected that some of the popping sounds she was hearing were semiautomatic rifle–related, though she couldn't be positive. She surely wasn't going to get up and look out her window to find out!

It was Christmas Eve–well, the wee hours of Christmas Day–and that is when, in many Central and South American countries, the Christmas celebration begins. At midnight, fireworks announce the beginning of the holiday, followed by the opening of presents and a huge Christmas meal. Wine and other drinks flow freely, allowing what inhibitions there may have been about noise levels to melt away. Sara kept trying to convince herself that, as she had been told, "It's not wrong, it's just different"; however, the longer she lay there, the more she was convinced that this difference was wrong!

Eventually the din subsided, and Sara felt her mind and body relax, sleep drifting over her. Though not fully asleep, she seemed to be at home in Michigan, and all was right with her world except for the loud knocking sound of a woodpecker against a nearby tree. The knocking became frustratingly louder and eventually roused her enough to realize that someone was at the door. She regretted leaving her visions of home behind but shook her head to clear out the dullness and glanced at the clock. Two-thirty a.m. Who could this possibly be? She hesitated, with safety concerns clouding her thinking, but then she heard Luz calling her name from outside the door. She got up, shouted for Luz to wait a minute, and threw on some clothes.

She opened the door to a loud but genuine *"Feliz Navidad!"* accompanied by the usual hug and kisses on each cheek. Luz, her friend from volleyball club, was one of the few local people with whom Sara had developed a deeper relationship. Why on earth was she here in the middle of the night? Sara offered Luz some *café*, and the two settled into a conversation about the holiday. Luz filled in some of the gaps in Sara's cultural understanding about local Christmas celebrations with her animated descriptions of the rituals her family enjoyed every Christmas season. As Sara began to share about her love of

Christmas, her family's traditions, and the reason for the celebration, she noticed that Luz became more and more pensive. She stopped Sara midsentence to comment, "*Hablas about Jesús like amigo*" in her best Spanglish.

Sara sat there, openmouthed, for a second. Was this going to happen? This was why she was here. Without having to think about it, her mind jumped into the training from Evangelism Explosion she had received years ago on sharing her faith in Jesus. As a Catholic, Luz certainly understood who Jesus was and what he had done, but to trust in him alone for salvation or to consider him a friend as well as Savior were new thoughts. Sara was continually praying as she talked, all her previous fatigue and frustration a distant memory. By 4:30 a.m. there was a new member of the kingdom. God had given Sara an unexpected Christmas present.

Though Sara had not received much formal training or education to prepare for her missionary experience, she had received the Evangelism Explosion training on leading someone to faith in Jesus. Thanks to that training, the window of opportunity in Luz's life became the doorway into the kingdom. Applicable education is usually beneficial in any field of work, including kingdom work.

One thing many teachers experience when serving at international schools is having to teach outside their main subject area. This happens because, for one reason or another, the school is short of staff when the school year begins, and so they may choose to fill the need with another teacher already on-site. This happened to me on multiple occasions, but thankfully, I had received training or had significant experience in those subject areas. Though music is not my vocation, it is undoubtedly my avocation. Having directed multiple choirs before arriving in Guatemala, it made sense that I help teach vocal music at the school. I had also run a business, so I taught classes on business. Be prepared to use whatever training and experience God has placed in your life.

Can God work through people without education and training? Of course, we see in Acts where at Pentecost he enabled his people to speak in languages they had not learned. In over fifty years of cross-cultural experience (some of that time as a child), I can say those miraculous happenings are rare. Also, getting a visa to stay longer-term in a country may require a degree in the area of work you anticipate doing. For example, a doctor friend of mine is doing work in the Middle East. His educational records and certified copies of all his licenses were required to get a visa to live and work in his service country.

Education may not be required in all circumstances, but it rarely hurts. Here are some things to think through in the area of educational preparation:

1. **Education never hurts.** Even if higher education is not required by the country you are considering or the agency that is pursuing you, it is rarely a bad idea. I have seen people use education as an excuse to delay their obedience, and in those cases, I would say, "Be careful.

God cannot be fooled." In general, education will broaden your knowledge and experience in areas of passion and future work. Potential education debt is a concern and should be kept to a minimum, if possible. Ultimately, the bottom line is obedience to the leading of the Holy Spirit.

2. **Tailor your education to your strengths and passions.** Trust that the strengths and passions you have are God-given. Don't get caught up in the belief that you should pursue a particular degree or certificate just because you think God may use it in another country. Use your time and money to prepare yourself to do what you love to do. Once, after I gave a young college student that advice, he responded, "What I am really passionate about is surfing, but how could God use that?" For the next fifteen minutes, I described surfing ministries I knew about and possible locations where it was needed but not yet being done. His parents weren't as happy about my advice as he was. I guess I didn't think that one all the way through! Please don't see this as hard-and-fast instruction. TESOL training and other courses like that are always helpful, whether or not teaching English is your passion. Get the sound advice of experienced people in your target country and from your agency.

3. **Education allows you to bring something to the game.** This is more important than you may think. Some want to get involved in cross-cultural work with minimal instruction and almost no actual work or ministry

experience. That kind of passion is commendable, but consider the following thoughts. Every person in a new culture needs help adjusting to just living in that culture, which takes away time and energy from someone already living and working there. Usually, this is done with love and joy. We have all been there and needed that kind of care ourselves. However, if the new person also brings with them little or no training and experience, they will need to continue to depend on others in the working out of what God has for them there. This mentoring or coaching is necessary and normal and given with love and joy. However, there is a point when that can become a burden and create a dependency that is not healthy or helpful. Proper, thoughtful preparation before arrival can minimize the time and effort needed to reach the productive stage of a new job in a new place.

4. Make decisions concerning an educational institution and course of study with your target country or culture in mind. Sometimes we think or are advised that a Christ-centered university education is the best foundation for cross-cultural work. While this may be true for people serving in most countries, it is certainly questionable when considering a limited- or restricted-access location. Most governments in those countries are sensitive to (and require) information about where you went to school and what you studied. If you have a Bible degree and want to get a visa into China as a "consultant," the government could honestly

wonder what your consulting focus will be. This is not just my thought. Multnomah School of the Bible chose to change their name to Multnomah University partly for this very reason. In today's cross-cultural kingdom work, nearly every degree or career focus will have tremendous potential for effectiveness. As I mentioned above, pursue degrees that reflect your passion. As in all things in this book, if you feel God directly leading you to a particular school, obey and leave the future up to him (since he is the only one with a grasp on that anyway).

5. **Bible education is helpful** when considering that a part of what you do will be related to kingdom growth. The ability to apply the Word of God to and through our lives is still critically important, but that ability can be gained in a multitude of ways other than through formal schooling. As in Sara's story above, her Evangelism Explosion training helped her take advantage of the opportunity that presented itself. Bible knowledge and understanding is also essential in carrying out spiritual warfare. Though spiritual warfare happens in every culture, our awareness of it is dulled in our home culture but heightened in a host culture. Being able to recognize those situations is paramount.

6. **Always combine educational experience with work experience** because often, the key to success in work is converting knowledge into action.

Education, specifically from a college or university, can pay great benefits when working in cross-cultural settings. It may even be required to be able to live longer-term in some countries. Once again, get the advice of those in active ministry, your agency, or your sending church leadership on what the best path for you may be. Remember also that obedience to the leading of the Holy Spirit is our baseline in all things.

CHAPTER 8

PHYSICAL PREPARATION

In which Sara finds that pride can't climb volcanos

Sara sat in the middle of the path. Nearly everyone else had gone on ahead. The quiet on the slope of the volcano was interrupted only by the beating of her heart and her heavy breathing. Her head was between her bent knees, and her eyes were closed. She was done.

"Are you sure it's okay if I leave you?" she heard Meg asking. "Sara! You are going to make it to the top, right?" Her mind could not bring her mouth to answer. It was currently occupied in the past.

Months before, Sara had stood above the school soccer field watching Meg running around and around and around it, working on getting in shape for their volcano climbing expedition in April. Though joining her would have been a good idea, Sara was sure she was in excellent condition. She had spent her life committed to being at the top of her physical game for volleyball in club, high school, and college. She was only one year removed from that, and now she played weekly with Luz and her other friends down at the park. Shrugging, she had sat down next to the high school seniors she was mentoring and rejoined the ongoing conversation about leaving the country, college plans, and, of course, boys.

The day of the hike was a beautiful one, like almost every day in this country. Not too hot. Not too cold. She had loaded her backpack with everything she thought she would need for the two-day trek, including lots of water, food, a sleeping pad and bag, pillow, tent, toiletries, some makeup essentials, and extra clothes. They planned to summit on the first day, spend the night on top of the dormant volcano (though volcanic steam still seeped through the ground), and come back down the following day. Some of her friends and schoolkids were going, and several local churchmen were also along to help carry equipment. As Sara hefted her packed-to-the-gills army duffle, she marveled at the locals who were slinging on mini packs that couldn't possibly contain more than a liter of water and a change of underwear. Several offered to help her by carrying her bag, but she declined politely, feeling pretty good as they started. Meg, of course, looked strong and under control. *"Probably should have joined her in training,"* Sara thought as they began the ascent.

Everything went well for the first half of the climb. They were in a good rhythm, having great conversations in English and Spanish, singing, and just putting one foot in front of the other. Around noon they stopped for lunch at a crossroads where the path divided, each path leading to the top of a volcano. Sara found a rock to rest her pack on as she slid out of the straps. Wow, she felt light as she pulled out her lunch and some water.

After an hour of food, conversation, and rest, everyone began to get up, don their packs, and head up the trail to the right. As Sara tried to rise, her legs refused. They had cramped up and felt like two lead posts attached to her waist. She tried shaking them out without appearing in distress. Finally, she was able to stoop under her pack, get into the sweat-soaked straps, and force herself to a standing position. Several people were waiting for her, and once they saw she was up and beginning to move, they turned and headed up the trail.

Each step felt like a marathon. Sara forced herself forward, but before she had gone a hundred meters, she motioned to the nearest local guy and asked if he would mind carrying her water. He happily did so, and she began again. It was as if she hadn't given anything away. A couple of steps later, she was giving him her whole pack. She held on to her pillow, though, wanting to be carrying something. Finally, as the last ounce of her pride drained away, she even gave that up and just tried to get herself to take the next step.

She made it another mile or so before she just collapsed in a heap beside the trail. Most of her companions went on, but Meg and a couple of local guys stayed behind with her.

"Sara!" Meg said again as if maybe Sara couldn't hear her. Sara forced herself to lift her head and smile. "You and Javi go on. I'll make it. I just need to rest a bit," she heard herself saying, though she was not sure at all that it was the truth. She forced herself to think about how she could make that happen, though it was a losing battle. Gabe would stay with her. He had her pack anyway. Maybe he could carry her up the rest of the way too. Wait. What? She hoped she hadn't said that out loud.

Meg left hesitantly, with a flurry of ultimatums about Sara making it to the top, which trailed off in Sara's mind as she drifted into an exhausted sleep.

After what seemed like moments of dreamless sleep, Sara opened her eyes. It took her a moment to remember where she was, but the fresh mountain air and the constant cry of parrots nearby brought her back to the path on the side of that volcano. Gabe sat there, patiently waiting for who knows how long. Sara got to her feet. She felt great. How could that be? Gabe's questioning look showed he was surprised as well. Sara smiled and grabbed her pillow from him. "Let's go!" she said, turning uphill.

This episode is from my personal experience. I was the one thinking I could make the volcano climb without training for it. Two of my children went on the climb with me, along with many others, and it was my sixteen-year-old son making me promise to make it to the top. He and his ten-year-old sister were bounding up the mountain. "Pride comes before a fall" would define my situation well. Like Sara, I eventually made it to the top and rejoined my children. The lesson I learned that day is deeply engrained in me.

Physical preparation for cross-cultural life and work is often overlooked. The truth is that living in another culture adds to the emotional and physical load you are carrying. Sara was in good shape in her home and at her altitude, but when faced with a task far beyond what she would have done in her home country life, her body was not up to the challenge. New cultures also bring new pollutants, new intestinal bacteria, and new strains of disease in addition to just altitude, temperature, and humidity. It is essential to be as physically ready as you can be. Here are some steps to consider as you prepare.

1. If you haven't done so recently, **get a full physical.** Cross-cultural living adds significant stress to your body. Changing laws in the United States may make it impossible for an agency to require that you have a physical, but consider one anyway as part of your own personal preparation. Tell your doctor what you are planning and, if you know, where you are going. This may help in determining whether you have any condition that needs special consideration.

2. Put some focus on **physical conditioning** just as you would spend time focusing on spiritual exercise. A missionary who is always dealing with physical issues due to lack of care is hindered in how God can use them. I am not referring to disabilities that God may have allowed in our lives to help us rely on him. I am talking about problems of our own making–neglect in caring for the body God has given us.

3. If you deal with **allergies** or have a **medical condition** that requires special treatment or food, do some research on your target location to determine how living there will impact you. Will you be able to get medications and

therapy if necessary? If not, what are the options used by other workers who minister there?

4. Part of physical preparation may include **vaccinations.** I would recommend three resources to determine what shots you need. First, find out if any vaccinations are required to enter the country or get a resident visa. You can do this by going to the country's visa site or checking with the visa service you are using. Second, check with the US State Department to see what immunizations they recommend. Don't freak out when you see the list. Finally, talk with expats you know who live in that country. They can be a voice of reality to balance the State Department. Ensure that you take records of all your vaccinations, especially tetanus/typhoid, MMR, COVID, and hepatitis.

It is easy to overlook the importance of being physically prepared for a transition like this. Just remember that we are integrated beings. If we are stressed or suffering in one area, all other areas are affected as well.

CHAPTER 9

EXPERIENTIAL
PREPARATION

In which Sara finds that it helps to know what you are doing

Sara sat in a new wicker chair in an empty room which to the casual observer would resemble the inside of a poorly outfitted coffee establishment. Her head rested in her hands, and tears of exhaustion streaked down her arms, leaving growing wet spots on her slacks. Each time the story played over in her mind, she tried her best to change it, but that was just foolishness. What was done was done. "Enough already!" she voiced out loud, but her mind wasn't listening. No one was listening; but the past replayed again anyway.

The idea had come to her nine months earlier as she sat in her local coffee haunt in the States reading the blurb on a bag of organic beans about how remarkable transformations were happening in communities because of the coffee business's global growth. *"I could do that!"* she remembered thinking. "I've worked in the coffee business," escaped her lips, to which someone near her had murmured "Congratulations" mockingly. Sara let the comment pass, grabbed a pen from her purse, and began to scribble some dreams on her napkin. That is where it started.

What had happened? She had thought it out, talked it out, and shared it with her friends and family. Many had joined her financially in the effort. She had made it to this country, learned the language and the culture, miraculously found a location, and set up shop with the help of some expats and locals. Things had started well, but then people started coming around who said they were from the "government," asking for money to make things legal. She had employed some volunteers, which she found out later was not lawful to do; something about having to pay any employee and expats not being able to volunteer because it took away potential jobs from local people. It had all snowballed from there, and now here she was with a closed coffeehouse, debts, and lots of shattered dreams and tears.

As Sara sat there, her feet began playing with the volleyball lying beneath the table. Volleyball was the shop's theme, because it was her love and the one thing from her past that connected her with her current community. Most of the friends who were helping her had come from her local volleyball family. She glanced around the lobby at the pictures she had chosen for the walls: smiling faces, fun times, and lots of children who were falling in love with the sport. Even in the despair of the moment, she couldn't help but smile.

"Why not volleyball?" she said out loud. She grabbed a napkin sitting on the table, pulled a pen from her pocket, and started to dream.

Sara's problem in this experience was not her desire to create a business that would lead to kingdom transformations in that city and its people. The problem was that she tried to start a business she knew very little about and had little or no training in. As she now launched out into a dream that included volleyball, a sport she had played since childhood and one that she had taught and coached in clinics and clubs, she was working in an area of strength and expertise. There would still be issues to deal with, of course. Starting and running a business in another culture is at least twice as hard as doing it in your home culture. Most local business ventures fail. Even more of them fail when begun somewhere unfamiliar to the entrepreneur. In this new venture, though, Sara had eliminated one huge element of stress. If there was one thing she knew and knew well, it was volleyball!

My personal "coffeehouse" was trying to help local groups of believers write original music for their congregations. I had written and performed music for years, in and outside of the church, and I was confident I could help this happen in Guatemala for others. What I didn't have was any training in ethnomusicology, the science of local music–its form and function. After many months of trying on my own, I finally had to give up that dream. No matter how hard I tried, all the music I helped create sounded like me, like the music I liked and with which I was comfortable. Though the people I was working with were appreciative and encouraging, I later realized that they would never move forward on their own because it wasn't their own. It was mine.

Experiential preparation is critical in many areas, but it becomes paramount in starting a business. Here are some things to consider in getting experience to help do influential work in another culture with fewer misfires.

1. *Work experience*: It always helps to bring something to the "game" in the way of skills. Don't think job title; think what skills it takes to accomplish what you have done. Often God uses those skills in different ways for his kingdom.

    If you plan to start and operate a business, you should have had some experience starting and running a business in your home culture. No matter what you plan to do, teach, coach, or preach–whatever you want to accomplish somewhere else, it will always be more successful or come to effectiveness more quickly if you have experience in that skill in your home culture.

    Of course, God can choose to gift you on the spot with an ability you did not train for, but I have found this tends to happen in "on-the-spot" situations. When we have time to prepare, it seems that God would prefer to have us use that time in preparation, whether that be in school or at work.

2. *Ministry experience*: The absolute best preparation for cross-cultural ministry is ministry experience within your own culture. Monocultural experience has value, so get involved in your local church ministry or with

parachurch organizations near you who are working in your areas of interest.

Opportunities to gain cross-cultural experience are available in nearly all of our local communities. The world is literally at our door. You need look no further than the closest university, ethnic food store, or body of believers.

Short-term mission experiences are a great intro to what life and ministry are like if approached with that goal in mind. Let me say, though, that longer-term missionary life is more like your current "day-to-day" than it is like a short-term "busy every second" experience.

3. *Life experience*: You should know how to care for yourself before you move to another culture. Even if you are going to be part of a larger team who will be there to help you get your feet on the ground when you arrive, they are most likely not expecting to have to help you balance a checking account, go shopping, cook, wash clothes, or clean a bathroom. If you did not grow up doing these kinds of things and somehow avoided them in college, focus on them now. The last thing you want to be is a burden to your expat teammates, or worse, to the people of the country you are trying to lead to Jesus.

At least from a human perspective, applying experience to any given situation makes you more effective. There are exceptions, of course, and indeed you will need to contextualize to the new culture, but having previous experience will be an asset. I don't believe you need to set aside years to gain vast amounts of knowledge before getting started. Get experience as you go. Use your time wisely and be purposeful.

CHAPTER 10

CROSS–CULTURAL
PREPARATION

In which Sara finds that cross–cultural relationships are hard to navigate

Sara woke up with a start, sitting straight up in bed, wet with sweat even in the cool of the night. She glanced down at the right side of her bed. Empty. "So, it was just a dream," she said out loud as she exhaled a long, measured breath of relief. Her mind fought to clear away the confusion of sleep and remember what she had been dreaming.

The last thing she could recall was breaking into tears during a shouting match between herself and Shea's mom. Shea had stepped out to the store, leaving her alone with his mom for the first time, and Nita had lit into Sara with both barrels. Spanish was flying past her faster than she could grab, but the intent was clear. Shea's mom was not happy about their being married. Married?! How did all of this happen? Wait, she reminded herself, *it was just a dream*. She took another deep breath and blew it out slowly.

But it wasn't all a dream. There was a Shea, and his mom's name was Nita. Shea and Sara were in a relationship, and a serious one at that. How was that possible? She hadn't wanted this, but it had still happened. After her breakup with Chad, another relationship had been the furthest thing from her mind. As her head cleared, she rehearsed the past three months, searching for something she had missed, a clue to put this together in a logical way.

It was just after Christmas. Luz had come to faith in Jesus, and their relationship was growing deeper as Sara began to disciple her. Luz played with the national volleyball team as an outside hitter, and Sara had gotten to know many of the women on the team through various social events. Unexpectedly, one of the middle blockers had to return home from the capital, leaving an opening at that position. Through Luz, the coach asked Sara if she wanted to be part of the team for local competitions. (She could not play in international competitions because she didn't have permanent residency in the country.) She didn't even have to pray about this opportunity. This would give Sara an excellent chance to build on what God had birthed through her relationship with Luz and her growing ministry teaching volleyball clinics to children in the capital.

After a quick tryout, she was part of the squad and began practicing several times each week. Though Luz was as friendly as always, the other women on the team kept their distance. Sara couldn't figure it out. Maybe it was that she was North American, or that she was taller than everyone, or that her Spanish was so limited, but whatever it was, she needed to figure it out. Ministry was impossible here outside of relationships.

CROSS-CULTURAL PREPARATION

A month passed, and the date came for their first official away tournament. The destination city was a couple of hours away by local bus, and to save money, the men's and women's teams were traveling together. Sara was familiar with the men because both teams often practiced in the national gym simultaneously, and she had gone to a couple of their tournaments in the capital with Luz. It was evident that the team members were good friends, but once again, Sara seemed left out of everything.

A couple of empty seats remained as the driver pulled away, and one of them was next to Sara. She was alone in her two-seat bench because Luz had chosen to sit with her cousin, the backup setter for the women's team. Sara didn't mind. She could use the time to reflect on how to break into the group. Suddenly the bus stopped. The driver, anxious to get every peso he could for this trip, was picking up a couple of extra passengers. Sara's eyes got wide, and anxiety began to grow in her spirit. She had spent lots of time on buses with strangers over the last several months, but a two-hour trip next to the "wrong" person could try even the best missionary's fiber. The first person on the bus was an older man, disheveled and visibly hungover from the night before, or maybe even from earlier that morning. Sara was desperate but stuck. There was no "win" for her in this. She prayed silently for something to happen, though she didn't have any clue what that would be.

Suddenly, Shea, the setter for the men's team, hopped up from his seat and gently ushered the newcomer to it. After some conversation with the man, Shea made his way up the aisle to sit by Sara. She smiled at him and said "thank you" about fifty times in the next ten minutes. The two-hour trip flew by as she spent the time getting to know her "savior." Things clicked between them, and they got off the bus good friends. Immediately Sara noticed a significant change in everyone's attitude toward her. She was "in."

She knew without much thought that this all had to do with Shea. He had accepted her, and the rest of the two teams followed suit. So many great things happened as a result. All her local relationships deepened. Her Spanish grew by light years overnight. She had invitations to every event, all of which she attended with Shea. The possibilities for kingdom growth were huge, and it didn't hurt that being with someone filled the empty loneliness she continued to feel. Shea was benefiting from their relationship as well. No one in his friend group was "dating" a North American, which put him in a select category all by himself, and he didn't mind at all.

As the weeks passed, their relationship's win–win excitement began to have some nagging disconnects in Sara's mind. As she observed the relationships around her, she realized almost no one was married, even into their thirties. Most still lived with their parents, including Shea, and that had brought up another awkwardness. Evidently, she had done something to offend his mother, Nita, because she always seemed angry when Sara was around, and that was a lot.

Just yesterday, Sara had heard one of Nita's friends teasing her, which was very common in this country, referring to Sara as Nita's "*hijastra*," and Nita had not been happy about it. At practice that night, Sara asked Luz to translate, and Luz just began to laugh. "*Como ... married a Shea!*" She laughed again and bounded away.

"What?" Sara heard herself saying, but the word got lost in the sound of bouncing balls on the court. She and Shea were great friends, dating even, but a long way from engaged. Right? Did Shea think they were getting married? What had she done to give people that idea? At home, no one would have come to that conclusion at this point in a relationship, but then that was it, wasn't it? She wasn't at home.

This is one of Sara's longest chronicles and not very humorous, but it is real for so many young singles who take the gospel on the road. If you remember, when we joined her story Sara was in a serious relationship with Chad, which broke up because of distance over time. On top of that, living in a culture that is not your own and dealing with the constant stress of differentness can bring deep waves of loneliness. Sara was busy. She had friends. Though she had several setbacks during her time there, she also had some successes. From the outside looking in, she was doing fine. On the inside, however, the unseen effect of cross-cultural living had a life-changing impact. Her resulting loneliness broke through her defenses and led her into a relationship with Shea. In her saner, more objective moments, she knew she was using him and also knew he was using her. This was not a relationship based on love but on mutual emotional need and convenience.

Though I had spent eleven of my early years growing up overseas, thriving in another culture as a child, I found that experience did not immunize me from experiencing culture shock as an adult missionary. However, it did delay the effects that monocultural people feel in six months for about six years. I found myself experiencing fits of anger and irrational thoughts and actions. I remember my dad telling me before we left that I might discover I had a temper. Like other advice my dad gave me about missions that I disagreed with, I just shrugged it off, but as usual, he was right.

Living cross-culturally affects everyone, and though you cannot altogether avoid it, you can prepare yourself for it and possibly lessen its effects on you. Here are some things to consider in preparation.

1. **Don't leave this off your predeparture prayer list: Pray** that God would prepare you and help you have insight into the effects of cross-cultural living on you. You may feel, in the middle of it all, that God does not hear you, but remind yourself with Scripture. Put those verses to memory so that you can bring them up no matter where you are.

2. **Create a supportive community,** both in your home country and in your host country. These should be people who know you well and are praying for you. They are people you have given permission to speak honestly, and sometimes bluntly, into your life. Be proactive in asking them to evaluate how you are doing. Meet regularly, personally or over the Internet, to share life. Commit to following their advice even if it goes against your emotions.

3. Learn as much about your host culture as you can before you leave to live there. I have mentioned this in other chapters, saying that connecting with people of that culture in your home community is a helpful step. Also, remember that culture is not born into someone. It is developed and learned while growing up in a place. Culture is influenced by **history and language**, so spend time in those areas. Culture grows out of **geography and climate**, so learn what you can about those things. Culture relates to **politics and the economy**. Spend time briefing yourself via the Internet and any international news available to you. Learn everything you can about the country and people group you are going to before you get there. Then, after you arrive, plan to spend lots of time discussing what you have learned with expat friends to see how it has impacted them. Develop relationships with local people of whom you can ask honest questions about what is frustrating you. Not only will this help your adjustment to a culture, but it will open doors for kingdom work as well.

4. Push yourself to have **experiences outside of your everyday routine** and then evaluate how you felt about them. Go to new places. Try new things. Eat new types of food. Learn a phrase or two in your target language and use it with others a lot. Take notes on yourself, because you will want to recognize thoughts and actions when living somewhere else.

5. Interview people who are living, or have lived, cross-culturally. Find out what their struggles were and how they dealt with them. This is most effective if they lived in your target country, culture, or people group.

6. Get training from www.knowledgeworkx.com if your agency does not require it or if you are going independently. Knowledgeworkx specializes in "intercultural intelligence" and is applied worldwide to help people live cross-culturally.

7. Short-term experiences in other cultures are helpful, including a vision trip to your target location. These are expensive, and their weakness is that you usually will not stay there long enough to get beyond being a tourist adventurer in your mind. Still, any cross-cultural experience is helpful!

Cross-cultural stress is a given when moving to a new country. It usually starts to show up at about six months and can last for the rest of that first year. It is not a forever thing, though. You will learn to adapt and live well within the new environment. It just takes time. Don't do this alone. Talk it out. Listen well. Trust others. Go deep in your relationship with God. He brought you here. He will sustain you.

CHAPTER 11

FINANCIAL PREPARATION

In which Sara finds that God does things his way

Sara and Meg hugged for a long time at the drop-off zone for the international airport. Both were crying. It had been an eventful year, and now it was over. Finally, Meg drew back and said, "Are you sure, Sara? I can't help but think this isn't going to work. I know that God is able, but to wait here at the airport? It's not safe."

"I know this is what God wants me to do, Meg, but thanks for your concern for me now and over the last year. You're the best!" Sara replied.

"Why won't you let me buy you the ticket? You can pay me back later. It's not a big deal. I have the money available," Meg pleaded.

Sara paused for a moment. This sounded like a great idea, but also like the easy way out. Shouldn't she trust God to provide, not rely on Meg yet again? "No, Meg. God will provide. I know this is weird, but I feel it is what God wants. Thanks again, though."

Meg nodded. "You're right. He is able. We will be praying that God meets you right here in a special way. If you need me, you know where home is, right?"

They hugged again, and then Meg got in her car, started it up, and drove away, disappearing in the usual cloud of blue diesel smoke. Sara smiled as she thought back on the first time she had seen Meg drive away like that. And how could she have not figured out that "tinta" was dye and not soap? Wow, that seemed like so long ago. She shook her head and pushed open the door into the terminal.

The airport was busy, as usual, even this early in the morning. Sara wondered where she should wait for this provision from God. As she glanced around, looking over the many heads surrounding her, she found the restrooms, always a good thing to locate. She pulled out her local driver's license and smiled. "A urine test for a driver's license," she said out loud, shaking her head.

Sara decided that hanging out near the ticket and check-in counters would be her best opportunity to be contacted. As she was settling in, leaning against the cool concrete wall, she saw what appeared to be a sizeable short-term team from the United States getting ready to check in for their flight home. Several of them looked over at her. She met their eyes and smiled, wondering what their stories of challenges and God's faithfulness might be. Sara prayed as she watched, thinking that maybe this group might have an extra ticket. The group finally got all their stuff together and checked onto the plane.

Their leaders herded everyone downstairs to departures. A few of them waved. Sara waved back.

The hours passed slowly. It seemed like Sara had watched half of the country's population come or go. Still no special provision from God, but one thing was certain at that moment: she was hungry. Nearly all the restaurants were on the lower floor, so Sara headed down the escalator. As she tried to decide what to eat, she remembered an *Amazing Race* episode where a couple had lost all their money and begged to get the bus fare to the next location. Maybe that is what she was supposed to do. She had seen God work in beautiful ways in the last year, but she had to put some skin in the game too. Deciding to pick a restaurant based on the presence of people to approach for money, Sara fervently prayed that God would direct her to the right place.

There, sitting at a table in the dining area of a local food establishment, was an older couple about Sara's parents' age. She decided to approach them, and though she was afraid, it wasn't a worse fear than she had experienced asking for support to get here in the first place. She got in line, ordered her lunch, and prayed as she waited to receive it. With her loaded tray in hand, she approached the couple and asked if they would mind if she joined them. They smiled and welcomed her to their table, though there were empty tables in the area.

They chatted about everyday things, who they were, where they were from, and what they were doing in the country. As it turned out, these two were Christians and were also returning to the US. They had been on vacation. It was Sara's turn to reveal her purpose there. She smiled and silently prayed as she began.

After a short autobiography of the last year, she swallowed and let her request fly. "I'm also on my way home," she said, "but for a variety of reasons, I don't have any money for my ticket. You two wouldn't be able to help me, would you?" Compassion swept across the faces of the older couple. Sara grew hopeful.

"Honey," began the woman just as Sara's mom would have, "we would love to help, but we aren't in the position to be able to do that. We are on a fixed income and have just spent all our extra money to take this trip. I am sure God will provide, though. Let us pray for you before we leave."

Sara forced a smile and thanked them for their willingness. They closed their eyes in that crowded place and prayed, Sara that God would give this couple a safe trip home and they that God would provide in a miraculous way for Sara's ticket. They bused their table, hugged, and said goodbye.

As she made her way back to the upper floor, tears welled in her eyes. That should have been the moment. Everything was happening the way she thought it might, until the end. Why had that not worked? What was God doing?

Once again, she scanned the crowd at the ticket counters for no logical reason and then leaned against the wall in her chosen spot. The afternoon passed rather quickly, and nothing of note happened. To be honest, Sara was defeated and her faith that God would provide money for her that day was all but gone. As the afternoon turned into evening, she began to wonder what to do. She couldn't stay there. She didn't want to go back to Meg's. What would she say? How foolish she had been. However, going back was all she could do, so she walked outside with her bags and got into a taxi.

FINANCIAL PREPARATION

Standing outside the gate at Meg's flat, Sara sighed and pressed the intercom button. Hearing Meg's voice crackling over the speaker brought warmth to Sara. Fear melted away. It was only seconds before Meg unlocked the gate and they were hugging again. Sara wept. It had been a long day. After some minutes, Meg helped her compose herself and said, "There are people here. We've been praying for you." Sara wiped her eyes and gave Meg a questioning look. Meg just smiled and grabbed her hand, leading her up the steps into the formal living area.

The well-lit room was full of people, and as Sara walked in, smiles broke out on many faces. Hugs and kisses were abundant, but finally the commotion subsided. Luz was there, and she had Sara sit next to her, not wanting to let go of her hand. "What happened?" she asked, which was the question on everyone's mind. Sara hesitated. This was not a happy tale, but finally, she began. When she got to the part about praying with the American couple, Meg held up her hand to interrupt Sara.

"What time was that?" she asked.

"About two," Sara answered.

Meg beamed. "Right at that time, I was praying for you. God spoke to me and led me to call everyone together. Within an hour, we were all here praying. I set a bowl out on the table, and everyone chipped in to help you with whatever money God led them to give. There is more than $900 here. That should be more than enough. Sara, God did provide, just not in the way you thought he was going to."

Sara was crying again. She was humbled. She was thankful. She was embarrassed. She was tired. Luz held her until she could speak. She thanked everyone, smiling weakly. What more could she do? Finally, people took their leave and said their goodbyes, knowing that Sara would be getting on an airplane the following day. Luz was the last to leave. She was the one crying now. *"No forget me, Sara. Te amo!"*

Financial preparation for missions is undoubtedly the most difficult challenge for most people. Our story was not much different. Having been raised in a missionary family, I had seen my parents raise money. It didn't seem too hard at the time. I was pridefully sure I could do it. That pride led to my complete failure. After about eight months of trying everything I could think of and hitting my head against the wall, I surrendered. We still believed that God wanted us to be missionaries, but I was done trying to raise money. A strange thing happened. At the time, we were assigned to Germany, but the team there called our headquarters and recommended that we not go there.

The timing just wasn't right, they had said. Maybe we should have been crushed by this, but instead, we were overjoyed. God was at work. True, we now didn't know where we were going, but at least he had closed the door to where we thought we were going. For a month, while we awaited our next assignment, we just praised God that he was making a way for us. We didn't meet with anyone. We didn't ask for money. Honestly, we didn't have anyone left to ask. That month, the month we did nothing but praise God for who he was and for what he was doing, we received three times the largest amount we had received in any month up to that point!

Everyone's funding story is different, but God's fingerprints are all over each one. If he leads you to get involved cross-culturally, he will provide in his way and in his time. Here are some things to consider in preparing for his provision.

1. Pray. Raising money feels so physical, and indeed, there is a very real-world part of it, but when it comes to God's business and his provision for his work, prayer is priority number one. Though prayers of petition, like asking God to provide the money somehow, are appropriate, they are not the end game. Where you need to go in prayer is a more profound place with the source of your vision and your provision. God's direction becomes more evident as we get to know him better and understand how he made us more fully. Learn to listen to the Holy Spirit and to recognize his leading in your spirit. I wrote a lyric once that still guides me today.

    Let my thoughts be thy thoughts
    Our spirits be one
    Let my will be thy will
    And thy will be done

2. Praise. As I mentioned above in our story, praise played a huge role in seeing God provide. We began praising God when the situation looked its worst. Praise changes our focus and attitude. Instead of seeing the need, we see the source of all provision. Instead of seeing the impossible, we remember the faithfulness of the God for whom nothing is impossible. When the night seems

darkest, focus on the light inside you and inside those around you. We have met and counseled many defeated warriors. We all face challenges beyond our ability, and we all fail. What we do next is what defines us. Let that next thing be praise.

3. Serve. As we walk the path of discovering God's provision for our next thing, we should not neglect serving others, the current (and always) thing. Some people define this as helping others understand that there is a reward in giving, and there is undoubtedly some biblical support for that. However, sometimes we give and we don't get more back. We should give because God has asked us to, not because of the desired reward. Serving others involves sacrifice. As we demonstrate sacrifice in our service to people, they may see God's leading for them to sacrifice for others as well.

4. Give. If you are not actively and financially supporting missions, I might question your belief that God is leading you into that type of ministry. Once again, this is not a give-to-get, cause-and-effect kind of thing. Your generosity should be in direct obedience to God's leading. This is what you will ask of others. If they sense that God is leading them to support you, you hope they will be obedient. If not, then you expect them to follow his leading toward supporting some other work or person. Obedience is our life's calling, no matter where we live or how we serve the kingdom.

5. Commit. Nothing done with a divided heart is done well. If you genuinely believe that this is what God is asking you to do, then go all in and give it everything you are. I refer you to the prerequisite for this book. Is God asking you to do this? If so, obey with your whole heart. If not, pursue him more deeply to find out what he desires from you at this point.

6. Champions. Don't go this alone. Even before you take your first steps along this path, find others who will be your champions along the way. These people are with you no matter what. They will encourage you when you are discouraged. They will correct you when you get off track. They will introduce you and endorse you to others with a similar heart for the ministry God is calling you to. They may or may not financially support you, but they are worth so much more than money on the journey. Seek them out and ask them to be members of your "mighty warriors" team (see 2 Samuel 23).

7. Stories. Finally, talk to those you know who have walked the path before you. If your church supports missionaries, find out how to connect with them and ask them how God revealed himself in their story. As I said at the outset, the stories you hear will be unique, but God's fingerprints will be evident on each one. Look for the underlying truths about the God you serve. Align that with how you have experienced him working over the years of your life. You will see the parallels.

Entire books have been written about raising money for missions, and my purpose is not to give you an exhaustive resource but to encourage you to take reasonable first steps. Many agencies have programs to help you raise money. Some will be internal, and some may be with third-party organizations. If you join an agency that does not have support-raising help, ask them whom they would recommend you contact. If you still come up empty, contact me.

EPILOGUE

Sara looked at the package in her hands. It was from Luz. She and Luz were meeting virtually every month as Luz continued to grow in her living faith in Jesus, but why would she send something like this? It wasn't a large box, but one that had no doubt cost Luz several hundred pesos to send. Sara sat and opened it carefully.

The first thing that confronted her was a very familiar aroma, that of freshly roasted coffee beans. Sara recognized the packaging as from the plantation she had partnered with during her doomed coffeehouse ministry attempt. The business had failed, but certainly not because of the coffee. It was wonderful! She held the bag up to her nose and inhaled deeply. Warmth poured over her, and she just sat for a moment, full of memories.

She put the bag of coffee down and pulled out a newspaper clipping. Her eyes were drawn to the picture of a large group of children, several holding volleyballs. The caption read, *"El Impacto de Deportes en la Juventud." The impact of sports on youth*, she translated to herself. Wait. She looked closer at the picture. It was of her kids. She was sure of it. The work Sara had started over a year ago, reaching out to street kids using volleyball, was still going on and was working! Luz had written on the back of the article, "You make a difference here, Sara!"

Tears welled up in Sara's eyes, and she quickly wiped them, not wanting their moisture to smear the newsprint. She didn't take time to read the article because she was now opening a card, the next thing out of the box. It was a thank–you card with a picture inside. The image was of Luz and her entire family standing in front of their Christmas tree in the wee hours of Christmas Day, happy smiles on every face. On the card Luz had written, *"Mi family total is evangelico!"* This time Sara could not stop the tears. They flowed freely down her face and past the smile on her lips. Luz's whole family was following Jesus.

It took some time for Sara to move on to the last item in the box. It was a note. The handwriting was different, but she recognized it immediately. The message was from Shea.

She gazed out into the distant nowhere, her mind trying to make sense of her many thoughts and emotions. Sara had thought she had moved on from her relationship with Shea, but apparently, there was more to process. She forced her eyes back to the note. It was in Spanish, but she was accustomed to his lilt and word choice. The intent flowed effortlessly from his words to her mind. He missed her and was sorry he had

EPILOGUE

let her go without saying goodbye. Luz had invited him to her church, and he had gone once or twice. Shea had asked Luz to explain the difference between her new faith and his, but she had recommended that he write this note instead. Sara smiled. She knew what Luz was up to, and she was thankful, though that emotion surprised her.

Sara skipped to the end, as was her habit with letters. *"Hablemos pronto! Besos y abrazos. Shea"* Was Shea going to call her? Is that what "We'll talk soon" meant? Indeed, he could. Luz had her contact info. She didn't put much importance on his "kisses and hugs" closing. Everyone said that to everyone, all the time. Still, it would be good to reconnect. Her phone buzzed. It was Luz.

Sara's story is a pretty sad one, and I didn't even go into having a car stolen, being held at gunpoint on top of a volcano, and having the child of a close friend kidnapped. I don't feel too bad for Sara though. She's fictional, and the stories I have used to lead us into the topics of this book happened to various people over many years. No one lives a life quite like Sara's when working overseas. Don't be afraid, because God's love leaves no room for fear. Just obey.

In this epilogue, I wanted to reveal the rest of her story. Though Sara struggled through her one year of service overseas, she had a significant impact that remained after she left. As you know, God brings the increase to his kingdom. We are honored and humbled to be part of what he is doing. To capsulize Sara's experience, we can look at 2 Corinthians 12:9:

"My grace is sufficient for you, for my power is made perfect in weakness." Therefore, I will boast all the more gladly about my weaknesses, so that Christ's power may rest on me. (NIV)

Congratulations on reaching the end of this challenging little book on preparation for cross-cultural life and ministry. I hope it will be a help as you take steps forward in obedience to God's leading. At the risk of being redundant, allow me to revisit the most critical things I want you to take from this book.

1. No matter how God is leading you, commit yourself to obey him.

2. Make prayer your highest priority.

3. Preparation can't guarantee that you won't deal with difficulty or embarrassment in your transition to another culture. The real stories I have used in this book happened mostly to experienced people. However, preparation can help you avoid some common pitfalls and lessen the impact of those that cannot be avoided.

4. Preparation doesn't have to be expensive financially and can be done right where you are.

5. Knowledge is your best friend in cultural transition. Commit significant time to research.

6. Ask questions freely of those who have gone before you. Learn from their experiences.

7. Don't go it alone. Form a team of champions to support you and hold you accountable in your obedience.
8. And finally, don't give up. Learn to wait on God's plan and timetable.

More resources are available at

https://www.prepareforimpact.life

and that is also the best way to contact me. I am looking forward to serving together!